Trust

Biblical Truth Simply Explained

Baptism with the Holy Spirit
Jack Hayford

Biblical Meditation
Campbell McAlpine

Blessings and Curses
Derek Prince

Deliverance
Bishop Graham Dow

Forgiveness
John Arnott

The Holy Spirit
Bob Gordon

Prayer
Joyce Huggett

Rejection
Steve Hepden

Spiritual Protection
Lance Lambert

The Trinity
Jack Hayford

Trust
Tom Marshall

Worship
Jack Hayford

Trust

Tom Marshall

Chosen Books
A Division of Baker Book House Co
Grand Rapids, Michigan 49516

Published in the USA in 2004 by Chosen Books
a division of Baker Book House Company
P.O. Box 6287, Grand Rapids, MI 49516-6287
www.bakerbooks.com

Originally published under the title *Explaining Trust* by Sovereign World
Limited of Tonbridge, Kent, England

Printed in the United States of America

Library of Congress Cataloging-in-Publication Data
Marshall, Tom, d. 1993
    [Explaining trust]
    Trust / Tom Marshall.
        p. cm. — (Biblical truth simply explained)
    Originally published: Explaining trust. Tonbridge, Kent, England :
Sovereign World, 1992.
    ISBN 0-8007-9367-6 (pbk.)
    1. Trust—Religious aspects—Christianity. 2. Trust—Biblical teaching.
I. Title. II. Series.

BV4597.53.T78M33 2004
241'.4—dc22

                                                            2003060281

Notes for Study Leaders

This book is a biblical and practical study of trust. The teaching is not just meant to be discussed—it is to be responded to. Five study questions at the end of each chapter are designed to help members of a study group think about and engage personally with this subject.

As a leader, you will need to balance the needs of individuals with those of the whole group. Don't be surprised if different opinions and feelings arise during the study, particularly when answering certain questions. It is wise not to get side-tracked, devoting too much time to one person's thoughts. Instead, enable everyone in the group to share and to respond to the positive message of the book.

This study should take place in an encouraging and receptive atmosphere, where group members feel able to share openly. Encourage group members to read one chapter prior to each meeting and think about the issues in advance. Reviewing the content of the particular chapter at the meeting will refresh everyone's memory and avoid embarrassing those who have not managed to do the "homework."

Praying together and asking for God's help will help each person to take hold of the truths presented. Our hope is that as readers explore this vital theme of trust, they will experience increasing fruitfulness in their lives. May God bless you as you study this material yourself and lead others in doing so.

Contents

Introduction:
The Importance of Trust

Trust is essential to life in society. Social interaction and organization would be impossible in a world where nobody could be trusted. We need a dependable and predictable environment to be able to order our lives with reasonable confidence. Because of that, we want and need the world, and the people in it, to be trustworthy.

We come into this world trusting. Suspicion and mistrust are attitudes we learn later, and they are always learned through painful experiences. They change the innocent eyes of childhood into the wary, watchful eyes that look out of so many older faces.

Trust is a necessary condition for the formation of any type of personal relationship. Can you imagine someone saying to you, "I would really like to be your friend, but don't expect me to trust you"? You might say, or at least think, "Go find yourself another friend!"

The more important the relationship is, the more vital trust is to that relationship. If I am part of a climbing team and am hanging over a cliff by the end of a rope, the primary concern in my mind regarding the person on the other end of the rope is not whether or not I like him or her, but whether or not I can trust him or her. My life may depend on that.

The more intimate the relationship is, the more costly the commitment of trust becomes. Thus, it lies right at the heart of relationships like marriage, parenthood and leadership.

Because all relationships involve trust, it is necessarily involved in our relationship with God, because we relate to God in much the same way as we relate to other people. So we see that faith is not a condition that God has capriciously laid down; both faith and trust are natural and essential to our relationship with Him.

But What Is It?

Although trust is so vital, its nature and its requirements are by no means well known. In the Church we call it "faith," and we publish hundreds of books every year to extol its virtues, praise its achievements and try to explain its dynamics. Faith, or more of it, is widely regarded as the key to health, happiness, prosperity, success, fruitfulness and spiritual maturity. But to acquire it or develop it remains, to most Christians, a tantalizing mystery.

It would be well worth our while to gain some clarity on what trust and faith really are, before we get too far in our discussion of their roles in personal relationships. To do so, we will have to get behind or beyond the slogans, religious or otherwise, such as "Have faith," "Trust me," "Only believe" and so on.

What is trust? What are its conditions? What happens when you trust? How do you build trust? How is trust broken or lost? When it is lost, can it be restored? These are basic but vital questions whose answers we cannot assume or take for granted as being common knowledge. Some of the answers you will find in the following pages.

1

The Nature of Trust

We will begin by attempting a simple definition of the nature of interpersonal trust:

▶ *To trust someone is to voluntarily make yourself dependent on that person for some outcome or other, or for some result or consequence.*

Note the following very important characteristics that describe the situation we have defined as trust.

Trust Is a Choice We Make

Trust or faith cannot be forced on us. If we are going to trust people or put our faith in them, we must do it voluntarily. If people are told by their leaders, "You will just have to trust us in this," such trust is by no means assured. Even if control of the outcome is out of the people's hands and they have no option but to leave it in the hands of the leaders, doubt or mistrust is very likely.

Trust Is an Attitude

Attitudes are what govern our life and behavior. Attitudes are different from beliefs because beliefs are purely cognitive, and we do not generally act on the basis of our beliefs alone.

Trust as an attitude has three components:

1. A *cognitive* element—that is, we are convinced that the other person is trustworthy. Abraham was "fully persuaded that God had power to do what he had promised" (Romans 4:21).

2. An *emotional* element—that is, we feel confident about trusting the other person. "Faith is being sure of what we hope for and certain of what we do not see" (Hebrews 11:1).

3. A *volitional* element—that is, we act on it. Like Peter, we have to get out of the boat and walk on water (Mathew 14:29). "Faith without deeds is useless" (James 2:20).

To Be Trusted Is a Responsibility That We Voluntarily Accept

We cannot accept people to be trustworthy unless they know and accept the terms of that trust and the responsibility of faithfulness. In other words, there is a mutuality about it. Conscious and deliberate trust on one side has to be matched by conscious and deliberate trustworthiness on the other; conscious and deliberate faith on one side has to be matched by conscious and deliberate faithfulness on the other.

The Trusting Person Must Also Be Trustworthy

A little reflection will reveal why this must be so.

For us to be able to trust requires that the people we trust be trustworthy; that is, they take seriously their obligation to be reliable and faithful to us. However, they are unlikely to take on such serious and possibly onerous obligations toward us if they discover that we don't actually take such obligations seriously at all.

Moreover, if we do not take trustworthiness seriously in our own behavior, we will find it very hard to believe that anyone else will do so. Therefore, we will have great difficulty trusting anyone else.

The one who would trust must be one who is trustworthy.

The one who would have faith must be one who is faithful.

Trust Is a Risk We Take

When we trust, we let some of the outcomes of our lives go out of our sole control. They move partly or completely into the control of someone else, on whose faithfulness and ability we have chosen to rely. We cannot trust someone to do something and then decide to do it all ourselves. That may get the thing done but it makes nonsense of our claim to trust.

Trust Makes Us Vulnerable

To trust always involves our taking a position of vulnerability because we no longer have sole control over our lives. This is always a costly step, emotionally and psychologically, even if in no other way. There is no such thing as trust that costs nothing.

Because of this we will always find it easier to expect other people to trust us than for us to trust other people. Similarly, for us, it is easier for other people to be committed to us than for us to be committed to other people. This is the almost perennial failure on the part of many Christian leaders.

Trust Makes No Contingency Plans

The proof that we have trusted is that we make no contingency plans in case the other person lets us down. If we set up a fallback position, "hedge our bets" or provide against a possible letdown, it may be admirable discretion, but it certainly calls into question the level of our trust. If the other person learns of our contingency plans, he or she will soon realize that we don't really trust him or her at all.

Accepting Trust Involves Accountability

If I am trusted, and I have accepted that trust, I am answerable for the outcome, whatever it is. That means I have to explain any failure. This is why some people avoid positions of trust that are also positions of responsibility, because they do not want to be held accountable for the results.

Broken Trust Arouses Strong Feelings

Because trust involves vulnerability, strong emotions are always aroused when it is broken. When someone we chose to rely on fails us, there is a strong emotional letdown that is very painful. There is generally a lot of anger and hostility towards a person who is guilty of breaking our trust.

The root of such anger is actually fear. Our supposedly predictable universe is suddenly seen to be unreliable and undependable. This generates anxiety. We think, *If I can't trust a person like that, who on earth can I trust?*

Trust, Once Broken, Is Very Difficult to Restore

Trust differs from other virtues in its extreme fragility. Once trust is broken, it is very, very difficult to restore.

People may act unloving on one occasion, but we will tend to still believe that they are essentially loving. They may do us an unkindness, but we may still believe that they are really kindly by nature. But if we trust someone and he or she lets us down, we are likely to have a question mark about his or her trustworthiness for a long time to come.

The reason for this has something to do with the all-or-nothing nature of trust. It also has to do with the state of vulnerability that trust creates. When it comes to trust, you either do or you don't. You cannot partially trust, or if you do the uncertainty that it creates will cause extreme discomfort. Trust is like commitment—yes or no, in or out—and when it is broken, it is totally broken.

Broken trust is like a weak link in a chain—the whole chain becomes useless. "Like a bad tooth or a lame foot is reliance upon the unfaithful in times of trouble" (Proverbs 25:19).

Love is far more rugged and enduring than trust and can survive long after trust is lost. This creates enormous vulnerability. A person who is bound by love to a partner whom he or she can no longer trust is exposed to the possibility of intense hurt.

The restoration of trust, where trust has been lost, always takes time. Forgiveness for the breach of trust can be the work of a moment, but the restoration of confidence and the willingness to again take the risk of trusting is not the work of a moment. It may need patient rebuilding.

For this reason trust should be guarded very carefully, and the need to be trustworthy taken very seriously. "It is required that those who have been given a trust must prove faithful" (1 Corinthians 4:2).

Why Do We Find It Hard to Trust?

Some of the reasons why we seem to find trust or faith difficult may have emerged from what we have already discussed. Other factors may also be involved:

We Do Not Understand the Terms of Trust

Trust depends on relationships. You cannot safely trust someone whom you do not know or whose character or capabilities are unknown. To do so might be a dangerous presumption. "[The sheep] will never follow a stranger; in fact, they will run away from him because they do not recognize a stranger's voice" (John 10:5).

The basis and scope of trust must be mutually known and agreed upon by both parties. We need to know not only whom we can trust, but what we can trust them for. For example, to know and trust the integrity and honesty of a person does not necessarily mean that we can trust his or her advice on medical or financial matters.

Thus, the basis of our trust in God is expressed in His trust deeds, His covenants. In His covenant promises, He makes known not only His faithful character but also the precise terms on which He offers these gracious proposals to His creatures. Trust, like faith, is never a leap in the dark. It rests on knowledge.

Past Hurts and Disappointments May Have Made Us Wary and Cautious

We may have trusted in the past and been so badly let down that we are afraid of being hurt again. Or we may ourselves have been guilty of breaking trust and are afraid of further failure. What we have experienced is the fallen nature of a world that, having broken faith with God, now weighs heavily against trustworthiness or faithfulness in all its manifestations. "Many a man claims to have unfailing love, but a faithful man who can find?" (Proverbs 20:6).

In Trusting We Encounter the Root of Our Own Fallen Nature

The root of that fallen nature is the rebellious refusal of creaturely dependence on God the Creator. Instead we strive to

- Be independent,
- Seek self-sufficiency and
- Exercise sole control over our own destiny.

Trust strikes at the root of all three of these motivations, and therefore it meets resistance from all of them.

Trust means that instead of independence, we have to settle for interdependence. This means to be dependent on others in relationships and to allow others to depend on us.

Instead of self-sufficiency, we recognize our incompleteness without others. Instead of total autonomy, we allow the control of certain outcomes of our lives to go out of our hands and into the hands of other people.

Study questions:

1. In what ways is it a choice to trust, and to allow others to trust us?

2. Why does the author say that trust is an attitude, rather than simply a belief?
3. How is trusting a risky venture, involving vulnerability?
4. Why must we be trustworthy ourselves in order to trust others?
5. Is trust a difficult issue in your life? Explain your answer.

2

The Terms of Trust

To increase our understanding of trust and trustworthiness, we will examine some of the terms, qualities and character traits that are involved in trust and that give it content and substance.

The Qualities of Trust

Confidence

Confidence is "heart trust." It is trust that has been proven right so often that it has come to a state of settled conviction or assurance, regardless of what the issue is. The repeated acts of trust have produced a state of confidence. "Because God has said, 'Never will I leave you; never will I forsake you.' So we say with confidence, 'The Lord is my helper; I will not be afraid. What can man do to me?'" (Hebrews 13:5–6).

So also Paul writes to the Corinthians: "I have great confidence in you; I take great pride in you. I am greatly encouraged" (2 Corinthians 7:4).

Confidence is essential for intimacy. We confide only in those we can trust; therefore trust lies at the heart of the most intimate of our relationships. "The Lord confides in those who fear him; he makes his covenant known to them" (Psalm 25:14).

Loyalty

Loyalty is faithfulness at its most personal and most committed. It says,

- "I will be here in the bad times as well as the good."
- "I will be for you even when everyone else is against you."
- "I will defend you, even at cost or risk to myself."

Loyalty is an essential component of the most important and most intimate of our relationships. We rightly despise the "fair-weather friend" or those who desert commitments when the going gets rough. "A friend loves at all times, and a brother is born for adversity" (Proverbs 17:17).

Reliability and Dependability

To be able to trust people requires that we can rely on them to do what they have said they would do, without the need to check up on them to see whether it is being done or not.

Reliability and dependability are built up by faithfulness in small things. These small things often have a symbolic significance far beyond their immediate importance. "The first one came and said, 'Sir, your mina has earned ten more.' 'Well done, my good servant!' his master replied. 'Because you have been trustworthy in a very small matter, take charge of ten cities'" (Luke 19:16–17).

On the other hand, if a man is unreliable in small things, the judgment is likely to be, "If you cannot trust him in little things, what will he be like if we encounter a real crisis?"

Consistency

To be able to trust someone, we need to see predictable responses on his or her part. How can you trust someone who today is wildly enthusiastic about a project and tomorrow couldn't care less, or who one day treats something as a great joke and the next day gets furiously angry about it?

Similarly, it is difficult to trust an impulsive person because you are never very sure what he or she will do, or whether the person will leap into action on an inadequate consideration of information.

Consistency requires that we live by our principles and not by our moods. It requires that we act, not on whim or impulse, but on the basis of a rational or sensible consideration of the facts of the situation.

Faithfulness in Promise Keeping

Faithfulness in promise keeping means dependability of word. It means keeping promises or vows even when it is inconvenient or costly to do so.

Today the importance of keeping promises has almost disappeared from our culture, and the modern promise appears to have an unexpressed proviso, " ... provided it is still convenient and my feelings and circumstances haven't changed." With such conditional promises, it is no wonder that people's commitment also tends to be conditional. How can you commit yourself unreservedly to people who may back out of their promises if something better turns up?

Our ability to trust the Word of God rests on two very important truths.

1. *God never changes.*

> I the LORD do not change.
>
> Malachi 3:6
>
> Jesus Christ is the same yesterday and today and forever.
>
> Hebrews 13:8

2. *God's Word never changes.*

> I will not violate my covenant
>   or alter what my lips have uttered.
>
> Psalm 89:34
>
> Your word, O LORD, is eternal;
>   it stands firm in the heavens.
>
> Psalm 119:89

Honesty

It is very difficult to trust people when you cannot depend on them to tell the truth, or when you suspect that they are deceiving you in some way. "A truthful witness gives honest testimony, but a false witness tells lies" (Proverbs 12:17).

There are also ways of communicating that we may not recognize as being deceptive, but which create problems with trust:

- *Telling less than the whole truth.* What we say may be true, but it does not give the whole picture.

- *Speaking indirectly.* It is very common to say things obliquely or by inference, implying that the listener will "know what we are getting at." We are not really telling things the way they are, and it is difficult to trust a statement that has a hidden agenda or leaves other people trying to "read between the lines."

- *Communicating the facts but not our feelings.* In this case the person is left guessing about how we really view the matter.

Ways in Which Trust Can Be Damaged

The ways that trust can be broken are as diverse as the ways in which trust is created. The following failures are typical of the things that damage trust.

▶ **Breach of Confidence:** "You couldn't keep a secret."

If we open our heart to someone in confidence and then find that what we have shared has become common knowledge, it will be a long time before we take that kind of a risk again. Confidences are generally matters of intimacy and the breaking of confidences is very hurtful. "A gossip betrays a confidence, but a trustworthy man keeps a secret" (Proverbs 11:13).

▶ **Disloyalty:** "You took sides against me." "When things got bad, you weren't there as you promised."

Disloyalty is particularly devastating because it often occurs at times of critical vulnerability and exposure. When we most need the person's support, he or she is not there or has joined forces with those who are against us.

▶ **Betrayal:** "You sacrificed my trust for your own personal gain."

The difference between disloyalty and betrayal is that disloyal people desert their friends. But betrayers are traitors, acting deliberately against their former friends. Peter's denial of Jesus was disloyalty; Judas' false kiss in exchange for money was treachery. "Even my close friend, whom I trusted, he who shared my bread, has lifted up his heel against me" (Psalm 41:9).

▶ **Unfaithfulness:** "You broke your promise."

When we make a promise or vow, we voluntarily put certain restrictions on our own freedom of action to do, or not to do, certain things. What is more, we affirm or confirm our commitment in a deliberate way that is meant to be taken seriously. Such a commitment is relied upon by the person to whom we make the promise.

The assumption is that we will feel "bound" to keep our pledge and that the other person can trust us to do so. When we break our word, we shatter this trust. "They make many promises, take false oaths and make agreements; therefore lawsuits spring up like poisonous weeds in a plowed field" (Hosea 10:4).

▶ **Dishonesty:** "I can't believe what you say."

Our God is a God of truth, and that truth is expressed in His Son, Jesus Christ, the Word. Truth, the Word and faith are linked together.

Satan is a liar and the father of lies (see John 8:44). The devil, lies and mistrust go together. Lies and dishonesty are parasitic; they succeed only because they deceive people into trusting them as the truth.

▶ **Moral Weakness:** "I trusted your integrity, and you let me down."

Some people are unreliable because of sin and moral weakness in their lives. Often this is hidden and may only be exposed when it has become very blatant or serious, wrecking lives in the process.

When we think people are strong or when they hold positions of responsibility, we tend to lean on them for support or trust their moral integrity and self-control. If they collapse under us, we feel particularly exposed and defenseless. "You are depending on Egypt, that splintered reed of a staff, which pierces a man's hand and wounds him if he leans on it!" (Isaiah 36:6).

▶ **Uncertainty and Indecisiveness:** "You can't make up your mind."

When we trust we are seeking some degree of certainty, and look for it either in the character, the ability or the resources of the person on whom we are hoping to be able to rely. If we find that that person is doubtful, hesitating or vacillating, we will soon conclude that certainty is unlikely to be found there.

▶ **Unreliability and Inconsistency:** "I can't depend on you."

Inconsistent people sometimes turn up when they have promised to, and sometimes they do not. Sometimes they will fulfill a task, and sometimes they do not.

▶ **Moodiness and Emotional Instability:** "I'm not sure you'll feel the same way every time."

To be able to trust people requires that their behavioral and emotional responses are predictable. It means that the way they are likely to behave and respond in the future will be consistent with the way we have seen them respond in the past. Inconsistency and moodiness, which is emotional inconsistency, make such predictions difficult.

▶ **Lack of Self-Confidence:** "How can I be sure of you when you're not sure of yourself?"

Self-confidence is particularly important when the people concerned are leaders, fathers, husbands or authority figures. We are unlikely to place much reliance on the judgment or support of someone whose own sense of value is precarious. "What he trusts in is fragile; what he relies on is a spider's web" (Job 8:14).

▶ **Unfairness or Injustice:** "I can't get a fair deal."

When people's responses or reactions have been influenced by partiality, favoritism, discrimination, prejudice, dogmatism or other distortions, we can have little confidence in their decisions, because we never know the hidden agenda on which those decisions have been based.

▶ **Carelessness or Thoughtlessness:** "Your mind is not on what you are doing."

The person who is careless or thoughtless will let people down, not through deliberate intent but through neglect. It is the classic sin of omission as far as trust is concerned. To trust people, we need to be sure that they care about the concerns which we entrust to them, and will take thought about discharging the responsibilities they have accepted.

Study questions:

1. What does confidence have to do with trust?
2. How important are the qualities of loyalty, reliability, consistency and faithfulness?
3. Which aspects of honesty are connected with trust?
4. What do you think are the most serious causes of breach of trust?
5. Are any of the character qualities mentioned in this chapter particularly difficult for you personally?

3

Building Trust

Trusting people, or putting faith in them, can be both a crisis and a process. It is both a decision and something that emerges and develops gradually over time. We need to understand both aspects.

Trust Is a Decision

In any situation in which there is potential for a relationship to emerge, there is a period of tentative exploration and investigation. We experiment to see if the relationship will work. During that period of time, changes of mind, wavering and hesitancy are understood and permissible. But eventually there comes a point of decision when the question of ongoing trust has to be settled one way or another.

Courtship is one example. For a time there may be bursts of enraptured enthusiasm for the beloved, interspersed with agonized questioning and fears that it is all a horrible mistake. But eventually it has to be settled: yes or no, in or out. We know when the die is cast and the trust commitment is made. To change our mind or revert to uncertainty after that point would be disloyalty.

The same could be said of an employer who is hiring an accountant. He may vacillate between three people who could be the best person for this position of trust, and he may change his mind six times a day if he wants to, even to the point of rejecting them all. But once he decides and gives the job to one, he faces possible legal action if he changes his mind.

Trust Is a Process

But trust is also a process—it has to grow. One act of trust is not enough to provide it with enough impetus to survive the rigors of a relationship. The New Testament gives far more attention to the growth and building up of faith after we have come to Christ than it does to the initial act of faith that puts us into Christ.

This is arguably the biggest lack in teaching on marriage skills. There is a lot of attention to building love and understanding, but very little on how to build trust or to develop trustworthiness. If we gave it the ongoing attention and care it deserves, we would almost certainly have far fewer marriages foundering on broken promises.

How to Grow in Trust of Someone, While Increasing His or Her Trustworthiness

We have already seen that trust and trustworthiness go together. Because of this, increasing our capacity to trust is also dependent on increasing the other person's trustworthiness. Here are the important steps involved in this process:

Take Risks

There is no such thing as trust that costs us nothing. The cost is the vulnerability that is inevitable if we let real outcomes go out of our hands into the hands of another person.

Sometimes we say that trust has to be earned, and there is a certain truth in that. But we cannot prove that we can be trusted unless someone is prepared to take the risk of trusting us. That is the point of the parable of the minas in Luke 19. The nobleman's servants could prove their faithfulness or trustworthiness only because he first entrusted them with his money.

Play to Strengths Rather than Weaknesses

We must entrust people initially with things that they are good at and that they like doing. This is very important for parents who desire to bring up their children to be trustworthy people. Notice that the master in Jesus' parable of the talents entrusted differing sums of money to his servants, "each according to his ability" (Matthew 25:15).

Be Prompt to Praise

It is vital to praise success and to express confidence in the person whom you are trusting. We honor people when we trust them, especially when we then recognize them as trustworthy. "Well done, good and faithful servant! You have been faithful with a few things; I will put you in charge of many things. Come and share your master's happiness!" (Matthew 25:23).

Model Faithfulness

If we want others to be faithful and trustworthy, we must model the same characteristics in our own behavior and character. Children in particular learn by imitation, and they will prize trustworthiness as a virtue only when they see it practiced by those they admire most, that is, their parents.

We also have God's faithfulness and trustworthiness as an everlasting model and inspiration.

Build on Trust in Small Steps

Let the success of those you trust lead them into greater responsibility, but be sure to do it in small steps. The rule is to do things little by little, just as the master in the parable of the minas started by entrusting his servant to "a very small matter" before promoting him to something much bigger (Luke 19:17).

Be patient, remembering that your job is to build trust, not to test its limits. Therefore, do not stretch your own or the other person's capacity too far too fast.

Give Second Chances

If people fail you, give them another chance to succeed. Go back to where they succeeded once before and start again. Even when a person fails, be very cautious about accusing him or her by saying, "I trusted you, and you let me down."

This is particularly important as far as children are concerned. Trust is such a fragile thread at the beginning, that once you tell people that you don't trust them, it will be a long time before they will ever believe themselves trustworthy.

Do Not Talk Carelessly about Trust

If you are really testing people or trying them out for a job, do not tell them that you are "testing their trustworthiness." There is a proper time and place for trying people out, but this is not the same as learning to trust them.

If my boss says to me, "I'm trying you out to see if you can do this job" and I fail, all that we have found out is that I am unable to do that particular job. But if he says, "I am trusting you to do this job well," and then I fail, I have demonstrated that I myself am untrustworthy. This can destroy a person's confidence.

Never say to a child, or anyone else, "I trusted you, and you have let me down" if it wasn't crystal clear beforehand that he or she was acting on your trust. The other person must have a chance to understand and accept the trust placed in him or her.

How to Build Another Person's Trust in Us

Trustworthiness is built in very unspectacular ways, without panache or flair. Therefore it is more difficult for some temperaments to learn than others, not because it is hard but because it is painstaking.

Create a Climate of Trust

To create a climate of trustworthiness and dependability, we must:

- Be reliable and conscientious in discharging responsibilities and fulfilling tasks.

- Keep promises, even when it is inconvenient, irksome or costly to do so.

- Be consistent, acting out of principle rather than on whims or impulses.

- Be meticulous in keeping confidences, yet not promising confidentiality without knowing first what the confidence is about.

Be Honest
Honesty means sharing our feelings as well as our thoughts, so that there are no inferences to be made or hidden agendas to create suspicion.

Work on Character
Remember that a crisis does not create character. It only shows the character that is already there, which must be developed over time.

- Know yourself and the weaknesses that you must guard against.

- Don't give in to the temptation to take soft options or the easy way out. The right way may well be the more difficult of the options.

- Never compromise principles under pressure or for the sake of expediency.

Take Responsibilities Seriously
Take your responsibilities seriously. Ecclesiastes 9:10 says, "Whatever your hand finds to do, do it with all your might."

Be Cheerful
Keep a cheerful spirit. This means avoiding complaining in the bad times or falling into self-pity when the going gets

rough. It is very hard for someone else to have trust in us if we are always acting sorry for ourselves!

Study questions:

1. In what way is trust a decision?
2. How is trust a promise?
3. How do we increase our trust in others and help them become more trustworthy at the same time?
4. How do we help others grow in trusting us?
5. What aspects of this chapter have challenged you the most?

4

Restoring Broken Trust

Trust is a very fragile thing, and once broken or lost, it is very difficult to restore. In some cases, it may be impossible to restore broken trust apart from the grace of God.

Because the restoration of trust is such a serious matter, every breach of trust must be treated as a grave offense, even in what may seem to be a minor matter. One reason that trust can be so difficult to restore is that it is not taken seriously enough. To some people, if they break a trust, an apology and a promise to "do better next time" are all that seem to be needed to reinstate them as trustworthy.

Whether most people understand it or not, the process of restoration involves four stages, none of which can be overlooked.

- Repentance
- Restitution
- Redemption
- Reordering

Repentance

Repentance involves more than an apology or expression of regret for an offense. It requires a clear understanding by the offender of what he or she did, why it was wrong and what should be done about it.

For true repentance to take place, there must be a sincere acknowledgment that:

- a law of God has been broken,
- it is a righteous law and
- it was wrong to break it.

The law that was broken was that of trust or faithfulness. To break this law is an offense against the character of God, who is the One called "Faithful and True" (Revelation 19:11), and whose words are "trustworthy and true" (Revelation 21:5).

This acknowledgment of personal guilt must not contain excuses or rationalization. Rationalization attempts to find a reason for behavior that is comfortable for our egos to live with.

True repentance must involve a sincere intention to mend our ways and a resolution to be obedient in the future to the law that was broken. Repentance also requires faith that the offended parties are willing to forgive, not only as ones who have suffered personal injury, but also as persons who righteously resent the offense that was committed against the law of God.

It is extremely important that the offender not only offer sincere repentance, but also know that the one who forgives still preserves a high regard for the law that was broken. For that reason, forgiveness must be taken as seriously as repentance. The offense should not be dismissed with comments such as, "Never mind, it doesn't matter."

Restitution

Restitution is of vital importance, not just to forgiveness itself, but to the restoration of trust. Leviticus 6:2–6 provides clarification of this matter, requiring that if a man deceives his neighbor about something entrusted to him, cheats or swears falsely:

- he must return what had been entrusted to him or whatever he swore falsely about,

- he must make restitution in full, add a fifth in value to it and return it to the owner and

- he must bring a guilt offering to the priest for his atonement.

Restitution is not earning forgiveness. It simply makes amends or fair reparation for the wrong that has been done. It may even involve a public apology if the breach of trust has affected a body of people, or it may involve some voluntary service for the person who has been let down. In the case of a husband's marital unfaithfulness, for example, it may involve his voluntarily giving up certain freedoms or interests in order to spend more time with the wife who had been deceived, in order that their relationship be restored.

The purpose of restitution is neither punishment nor the earning of forgiveness, but the restoration of the damaged relationship. Therefore the form that restoration will take should arise out of a mutual agreement between the parties as to what is appropriate under the circumstances.

Redemption

There is only one place where we can find the resource we need to restore trust: the cross of Christ Jesus, which alone can provide forgiveness.

The death of Jesus was the ultimate expression of forgiveness. "Jesus said, 'Father, forgive them, for they do not know what they are doing'" (Luke 23:34). Not only does the cross secure our forgiveness, but it also makes available to us the grace to be forgiving. "Be kind and compassionate to one another, forgiving each other, just as in Christ God forgave you" (Ephesians 4:32).

The death of Jesus was also the ultimate expression of human trust. On the cross He let the outcome of His very life—and eternal destiny—leave His hands and be placed into the hands of the Father. He not only said, "I will put my trust in him" (Hebrews 2:13), He actually did it. "Jesus called out

with a loud voice, 'Father, into your hands I commit my spirit.'
When he had said this, he breathed his last" (Luke 23:46).

Because of this, there is at the cross a divine resource of trust,
injected into the bloodstream of humanity. It is what gives us
the confidence to trust again, even after our trust seems to
have been lost beyond human recovery. The cross can also
restore the capacity to be trustworthy again, when we—and
others—have lost all confidence in our ability to be worthy of
trust.

Just as forgiveness, and the ability to forgive, are supernatural gifts of grace and are received by faith at the cross of
Christ, so the redemption of trust is also a supernatural gift
of grace. This means that the willingness and ability to trust
again after trust has been repeatedly broken can be received by
faith. In the same way, the faithfulness that can make a
chronically untrustworthy person trustworthy is a supernatural renewal that is received by faith.

Just as salvation can make a rebellious person obedient, an
impure person pure, and a habitual liar honest, it can make
the unfaithful and disloyal person able to be trusted and
worthy of trust again.

But in this case, something has been added. Now our
trustworthiness is guarded by Someone on whom we can
depend, the One who is faithful and true. "I know whom I
have believed, and am convinced that he is able to guard what
I have entrusted to him" (2 Timothy 1:12).

Reordering

A final, vital aspect of restoration, too often neglected, is the
willingness to spend time rebuilding the flawed areas of our
lives. This work of sanctification follows the act of faith in
redemption. Deliberate discipline is necessary for this phase,
and it can often be a painful process to go through. "No
discipline seems pleasant at the time, but painful. Later on,
however, it produces a harvest of righteousness and peace for
those who have been trained by it" (Hebrews 12:11).

Often it is helpful to have a mentor, a spiritual friend who can be both compassionate and objective, and who can help you to see through some of the unconscious defense mechanisms you may have that are blinding you to the truth.

The specific situation that gave rise to the offense should be carefully examined to determine the answers to the following questions.

What Happened?

The first thing is to discover the nature of the failure. There may be one major or obvious breach of trust that has brought disaster, or it could be a tangled web of dishonesty, evasions, deceit and broken promises that needs to be patiently unraveled to establish the facts. Often there is much confusion in the mind of the offender that can make it difficult to see the issues with any degree of clarity.

Why Did It Happen?

Discovering the cause of the failure requires even greater care and insight. Is the person afraid to commit himself or herself, and if so, why? Does he or she get into difficult situations through thoughtlessness and carelessness and then seek the easy way out? Do character flaws need to be addressed, such as possible problems with lust, anger or untruthfulness? Does the person have an inordinate desire to be accepted, loved or admired?

The aim of answering this question is to enable the person to understand the problems that must be faced to prevent the situation from occurring again. At the same time, the person needs to have the courage to face the problems with the confidence that they can be overcome.

How Can the Situation Be Put Right?

It's essential to discover how the cause or causes of failure can be corrected. This means discarding dangerous or unhelpful patterns of behavior, and learning more consistent and helpful patterns in their place.

It may be that further ministry is needed for emotional or inner healing or to break any bondages that have been discovered. Remember that it is essential to go beyond understanding the nature of the problem, and begin to take remedial action.

When Will It Be Overcome?

Finally, we need to know that the weakness or failure has been overcome. Time is needed for the person's commitment to the prescribed courses of action to take effect. Time must also be allowed for God to deal with the person's life.

Encouragement is always necessary in this process, constantly recognizing the progress being made until the person can function with growing confidence in the areas where he or she has failed before.

Restoring Trust

People who have trusted but have been let down badly or frequently may eventually find that their capacity to trust again has been damaged. They may have been so hurt that it has become impossible for them to trust anybody again. "I believed; therefore I said, 'I am greatly afflicted.' And in my dismay I said, 'All men are liars'" (Psalm 116:10–11).

For such people, the grace of God that enables them to trust again may need to be accompanied by certain factors. These factors include the following.

Healing of Spiritual and Emotional Wounds

It is essential for the person to forgive the one who has sinned against him or her. This means letting go of all bitterness and resentment toward that person. If we hold on to bitter feelings, we effectively lock God out, because He cannot heal us while we cling to such negative emotions.

Jesus knows what it feels like to have His trust disappointed—His disciples abandoned Him and one of them even actively betrayed Him. But because He suffered to the utmost in all these ways, He is able to heal us of even the worst offenses.

Healing should always be ministered in the power of the Spirit. The Holy Spirit is the only One who can take the healing that flows from the cross and use it to bind up our broken hearts. "The Spirit of the Sovereign LORD is on me, because the LORD has anointed me to preach good news to the poor. He has sent me to bind up the brokenhearted" (Isaiah 61:1).

Examining Reasons for Broken Trust

It is essential to settle the circumstances surrounding broken trust. There may be important lessons to be learned from the situation, or moral or spiritual issues that should be addressed. For example:

▶ *Was trust placed presumptuously or foolishly?*

For example, was it done without knowing the character of the person who was being trusted? Were clear warning signs ignored?

▶ *Was trust placed for wrong or self-centered reasons?*

Was it to secure personal advantage? Was it to avoid personal responsibility? Was trust being given as part of a relationship that itself was wrong?

▶ *Was the trust itself idolatrous?*

That is, was it about trusting a person for things for which we are meant to trust only God? This may include unconditional, unchanging love and acceptance. If this is so, the basic fault of the offense does not belong to the person who failed to give what only God can give. "Cursed is the one who trusts in man, who depends on flesh for his strength and whose heart turns away from the LORD" (Jeremiah 17:5).

Encouraging Trust in God

A person's ability and willingness to trust God needs to be encouraged and reinforced. This is the rock beneath our feet.

When we put our trust in Him, He will never fail us. Even the most bruised and broken heart can find refuge in Him. "In God, whose word I praise, in God I trust; I will not be afraid. What can mortal man do to me?" (Psalm 56:4). "To you, O LORD, I lift up my soul; in you I trust, O my God.... No one whose hope is in you will ever be put to shame" (Psalm 25:1–3).

Involving a Trustworthy Person

For damaged people to safely venture out in trust again, they need a relationship with someone who is trustworthy. It is important to start small in this venture: The first steps may be tentative, but they must be safe. Give them time to become comfortable with the measure of trust they have been able to give. Let them set the pace. Build little by little, and don't go too far too fast.

Reinforce every successful step that is taken. If there is failure at any point, give encouragement and start again at the beginning, or wherever they can pick up the process.

Return their trust. For a person to learn how to trust again, it is easier if the person in whom he or she is placing his or her trust can be seen taking the same type of emotional risk.

Study questions:

1. Why is the restoration of trust such a serious matter?
2. What do true repentance and restitution involve?
3. What does Jesus' death on the cross have to do with trust?
4. What needs to be done to rebuild flawed areas of our lives?
5. Does your own ability to trust need to be restored? How can this be accomplished?

5

Trust and Faith

Trust and faith are very closely related. In fact, trust may be said to be an aspect of faith. But trust also has some special characteristics that can help to better illustrate the nature of our relationship with God.

We know that we will usually relate to God the way that we relate to others. True faith—which requires trust—means that we can let the outcome of the whole of our lives, including our eternal destiny, move out of our hands and into God's hands. It is a conscious choice that we make, and the proof that we have made this choice is that we have no contingency plans "in case" God lets us down.

Trust Rests on Knowledge

Trust with God as its object is never a leap in the dark. It rests on our knowledge of God's character (often referred to in Scripture as "His name"), and it particularly has to do with His faithfulness, truth and love.

We also base our trust in God on our knowledge of His ways and deeds—the consistent ways in which He works.

And finally we have God's Word, the revelation of His will and purposes:

> Those who know your name will trust in you,
>   for you, Lord, have never forsaken those who seek you.
>   Psalm 9:10

41

But I am like an olive tree
   flourishing in the house of God;
I trust in God's unfailing love
   for ever and ever.

Psalm 52:8

You answer us with awesome deeds of righteousness,
   O God our Savior,
the hope of all the ends of the earth
   and of the farthest seas.

Psalm 65:5

Trust in the LORD forever,
   for the LORD, the LORD, is the Rock eternal.

Isaiah 26:4

Here is a trustworthy saying that deserves full acceptance:
Christ Jesus came into the world to save sinners.

1 Timothy 1:15

We increase our knowledge of God by reading and reflecting on His character and ways, as revealed in Scripture.

We also cultivate our personal, firsthand knowledge of God through prayer and communion with Him. As we observe Him working in our lives and in the lives of others, our knowledge-based trust in Him also increases.

Trust Is a Settled State of Being

Trust has less to do with an act or a series of acts than with a state of being. Because it is based on knowledge of God's character, trust is at rest in the face of an uncertain future. This is so even when we cannot understand, or even when we misunderstand, what God is doing.

Trust leads to confidence and assurance in spite of baffling circumstances.

Though he slay me, yet will I hope in him.

Job 13:15

Though an army besiege me,
   my heart will not fear;

though war break out against me,
even then will I be confident.

Psalm 27:3

Blessed is the man who trusts in the Lord,
whose confidence is in him.
He will be like a tree planted by the water
that sends out its roots by the stream.

Jeremiah 17:7–8

Being confident of this, that he who began a good work in you will carry it on to completion until the day of Christ Jesus.

Philippians 1:6

Trust Waits for God

Because of their knowledge of God, those who trust in Him have the confidence to wait for Him. Even when it means waiting in the dark without evidence, it is possible to wait for His time to answer or intervene. "I will wait for the Lord, who is hiding his face from the house of Jacob. I will put my trust in him" (Isaiah 8:17).

Trust orients itself toward the future, and because its object is God Himself, it has the expectancy of good things. Trust is therefore not passive, but like hope, is an active openness to receive.

Surely he will never be shaken;
a righteous man will be remembered forever.
He will have no fear of bad news;
his heart is steadfast, trusting in the Lord.
His heart is secure, he will have no fear;
in the end he will look in triumph on his foes.

Psalm 112:6–8

Trust Must Be Wholehearted

There is only one way to trust, and that is with the whole heart. Because trust is essentially a matter of relationship with God, it is all or nothing. We trust completely, or we are not trusting at all. "Trust in the Lord with all your heart and lean not on your own understanding; in all your ways acknowledge him, and he will make your paths straight" (Proverbs 3:5–6).

God Trusts Us

Trust, as we have seen, is an essential element of all relationships. It is therefore not strange that we are expected to trust God, just as we are to love, honor and obey Him.

What we need to realize, however, is that God guards very jealously the integrity of our relationship with Him. This means that He also follows the necessary requirements that make up a relationship. He not only loves us (1 John 4:10), honors and values us (Isaiah 43:4) and understands us (Hebrews 4:15), but He also trusts us. "So then, men ought to regard us as servants of Christ and as those entrusted with the secret things of God. Now it is required that those who have been given a trust must prove faithful" (1 Corinthians 4:1–2).

The implications of this are staggering. God's trust is real trust. It is a choice He has made, and a vulnerability that He has accepted. In order that we might experience the joy of being trusted by Him, He has let some of the outcomes of His purposes go out of His sole control and He has shared them with us. He has made no contingency plans "in case" we let Him down.

That is why, in God's dealings with us, character is everything. His purpose is to conform us to the likeness, or character, of Christ (Romans 8:29), the One who is "faithful as a son over God's house" (Hebrews 3:6).

It is no surprise to find therefore that in the early Church character ranked above everything else. Character was ranked above charisma, gifting and ministry. "And the things you have heard me say in the presence of many witnesses entrust to reliable men who will also be qualified to teach others" (2 Timothy 2:2).

God prizes faithfulness and trustworthiness because they reflect His own character. Faithfulness and trustworthiness are essential to having a real relationship with Him. "If we are faithless, he will remain faithful, for he cannot disown himself" (2 Timothy 2:13).

Study questions:

1. What does trust have to do with the knowledge of God?
2. Describe some of the qualities of trust.
3. How do we know that God Himself trusts us?
4. Why are faithfulness and trustworthiness essential to a real relationship with God?
5. Do you reflect the character of God in your own life? Are there areas in which you do not do so? If so, what can you do to improve in those areas?

6

Trust and Marriage

Trust lies at the very heart of marriage. It permeates every aspect of the relationship and is required at every stage.

Covenant

Marriage is a wide-ranging symbol in Scripture for the covenant relationship between God and His people, and for this reason, the marriage relationship itself is a covenant. "For your Maker is your husband—the Lord Almighty is his name—the Holy One of Israel is your Redeemer; he is called the God of all the earth" (Isaiah 54:5).

In the new covenant, Christ is the Bridegroom (John 3:29), and the Church is His bride (Revelation 21:9–10). "Let us rejoice and be glad and give him glory! For the wedding of the Lamb has come, and his bride has made herself ready" (Revelation 19:7).

A covenant is a bond of personal loyalty between two parties. Therefore the heart of the marriage covenant lies in the vows that the parties make toward one another. They may say in the wedding ceremony, "This I vow before God." By these vows they have bound themselves to certain obligations. A covenant requires that we be faithful to the vows we make and to the person to whom we made them.

To break these vows is to be unfaithful. It is to "break troth," the solemn bond of fidelity and loyalty. The greatest sin that occurs when adultery takes place is the breaking of the covenant.

Grace and Faith

The basis of the covenant between God and human beings is grace on His part and faith on ours. The same takes place in the covenant of marriage; it consists of grace and faith.

Grace in human terms is simply doing good to someone else with no strings attached. Grace is the prerequisite for trust and creates the climate within which trust is possible. It is not difficult to entrust yourself to someone who does you good with no strings attached.

Faith in human terms, as applied to marriage, takes place when two people join themselves to each other in a lifetime commitment. They are trusting each other for their:

- Physical and material welfare and well-being,
- Spiritual health and well-being,
- Mental and emotional health and well-being,
- Sexual fulfillment and well-being and
- Social and relational fulfillment and well-being.

When we trust, we let some of the outcomes of our lives leave our own control, and we place it into the hands of the person we are trusting. The outcomes involved in marriage are among the most important, intimate and sensitive ones we will ever experience.

Risking these areas therefore creates great vulnerability. Isaiah wrote of "a wife deserted and distressed in spirit—a wife who married young, only to be rejected" (Isaiah 54:6). This vulnerability is why God has enclosed marriage within the security of covenant.

Submission

The overriding principle that controls all Christian relationships is set forth in Ephesians 5:21: "Submit to one another out of reverence for Christ." The following passage shows what this means for the relationship between a husband and wife:

> Wives, submit to your husbands as to the Lord. For the husband is head of the wife as Christ is head of the church, his body, of which he is the Savior. . . . Husbands, love your wives, just as Christ loved the church and gave himself up for her.
>
> Ephesians 5:22–23, 25

Submission involves trust because it includes yielding certain rights to another person. But the wife's submission is not unconditional because it has to be:

- As to the Lord, and therefore only to what would be in harmony with His character and ways, and
- To a husband who lives toward her on the basis of grace. That means that he must love her and give himself up for her in the same way that Christ loves and gives Himself up for His Church.

Trust creates responsibility. Therefore the husband is responsible and accountable for what is entrusted to him. This responsibility lies in two directions:

- As the head of his wife, he is responsible to his head, that is, to Christ Jesus the Lord.
- He is also responsible to the one who has trusted him, that is, his wife. He is accountable to her for what he does with the trust she has placed in him.

Intimacy

Qualities of trust are specifically applied to the sexual union of marriage in 1 Corinthians 7. When we trust another person, the outcome of some part of our lives goes out of our control into the control of the person we are trusting. Paul says, "The wife's body does not belong to her alone but also to her husband. In the same way, the husband's body does not belong to him alone but also to his wife" (1 Corinthians 7:4).

Because trust necessitates trustworthiness, the giving of each other in sexual union in marriage must be predicated on faithfulness.

The intimacy of marriage requires trust, or confidence. "A wife of noble character who can find? She is worth far more than rubies. Her husband has full confidence in her and lacks nothing of value" (Proverbs 31:10–11).

Openness

One of the most vital necessities to build trust in a marriage is walking in the light with one another. This means living in openness, sincerity and honesty. What inhibits trust is the knowledge, or suspicion, of hidden agendas, undisclosed secrets and concealed or suppressed desires or motives. You cannot trust someone whom you do not know, and you know a person only to the extent that he or she will reveal himself or herself to you.

But to walk openly with one another also requires trust, because it is when all of our secrets are out in the open that we are at our most vulnerable. We have to trust that our disclosures will be received fairly and compassionately, and that we will not be rejected because of what we reveal.

Openness generally develops gradually as a husband and wife discover that it is safe to trust each other with their secret fears and failings. And they find that vulnerability comes through openness, not through covering things up.

Study questions:

1. What makes the marriage relationship covenantal in nature?
2. In what way does the commitment of marriage involve great vulnerability?

3. How does submission relate to trust in marriage?
4. How is openness important in the development of trust?
5. Do you struggle with issues of trust in your marriage? What might God be saying to you about this?

7

Trust and Leadership

In the relationship between leaders and their followers, the most crucial element is probably trust. Generally, the more important the relationship, the more vital is the part played by trust.

In voluntary organizations such as a church, having the position of formal authority in leadership does not necessarily mean having the trust of all the people. When new leaders take over certain responsibilities, there is usually a time of uncertainty when people are making up their minds as to whether or not they can put their trust in their leadership. But sooner or later the decision is made. And until the leaders know that they have their people's trust, they may be able to maintain a measure of control, but they will never be able to truly lead the church anywhere of value.

All that has already been covered in this book also applies to the understanding of trust between followers and leaders, but note also the following particular considerations that apply to leadership situations.

Leadership: A Position of Trust

Leadership is always a position of trust. The superiors above the leaders may have entrusted them with the role or function of leadership, but with it comes the responsibility for results. One of the marks of leaders is that they are willing to shoulder responsibility.

The people who have committed themselves to the leaders or the leaders' goals have also exercised trust. As in other situations of trust, the people have let major outcomes (or what they perceive as major outcomes) leave their hands and pass into the hands of the leaders.

Trust is a cost of commitment, but few leaders give sufficient attention to the cost of the trust they are expecting from their people, sometimes even seeing it as a "right." Similarly, because they may not always realize the emotional and psychological vulnerability involved in such levels of trust, they often can be dismayed at the anger and hostility that is directed toward them if they are ever guilty of a breach of trust.

Furthermore, because leaders usually have more power and more information than others, they carry a greater burden of responsibility for the success of the relationship.

Trust and Accountability

Trust brings responsibility, and responsibility includes accountability. The question then follows, "To whom are leaders accountable or answerable?" The answer is, "To all those who have trusted them."

This means that in the church, for example, leaders must be accountable downward as well as upward. They are responsible to the people who follow them and have put their trust in them as leaders, as well as to the superiors who may have appointed them to their positions. They are answerable for the way they have led, because that is what people have trusted them to do.

Leaders are also accountable to God. Paul spoke to masters and told them to be right and fair "because you know that you also have a Master in heaven" (Colossians 4:1).

For What Do We Rely on Leaders?

We must be clear as to what it is that people are trusting in their leaders to do. Either explicitly or implicitly, it will usually be found to be the following elements.

Judgment

The task of leaders has to do with establishing the goals or objectives of the church or organization. The people, because they are less likely to see the future as clearly as the leaders can, trust that the leaders have gotten the goals right (that they know what they are aiming for), and set the right goals (the ones that are achievable with the resources that are available).

Note that people are trusting the leaders' *judgment,* not their *persuasiveness.* Because of this, it is always more difficult to trust new or untried leaders when there is no track record to go on.

Resourcefulness

People must trust the ability of leaders to handle whatever problems may arise in the future. They must also trust them to overcome obstacles that stand in the way of reaching the objectives of the organization.

Here again, confidence grows as leaders demonstrate their capacity to handle difficult situations. This is seen particularly in the ability to face problems without losing nerve or without moaning and complaining when things go wrong.

At other times, people's confidence, or lack of confidence, in their leaders is often a reflection of the leaders' self-confidence or lack thereof. Followers cannot be sure of leaders who are not sure of themselves, and they will find it difficult to trust the resourcefulness of leaders who are uncertain or indecisive.

Perseverance

People must trust that their leaders will "hang in there" in bad times as well as good, until their goals are reached or their objectives are achieved. Some leaders hand the reins over, or coincidentally get "called" somewhere else, if they think their venture is going to fail. They do not want their reputations tarnished by failure. If that attitude is in the leaders, it will create deep uncertainty in the followers even when things are going well.

Linked to the trait of perseverance is one's character, or moral fiber. In other words, true leaders have the ability to stand up under pressure without buckling or giving way. Note the emphasis given to character in the leadership of the early Church (1 Timothy 3:1–12 and Titus 1:6–9).

Integrity

As well as perseverance, there are certain essential qualities of character that people look for in their leaders. These include the following:

- Honesty will cause their word to be relied on. Their message should not be different for different people, and the whole truth must always be told.

- Fairness means that leaders are just and equitable in their treatment of people. They will avoid favoritism, partiality and discrimination.

- Openness in admitting mistakes or errors of judgment is an essential quality of good leadership. This means confessing mistakes without rationalizing, making excuses or evading responsibility by "passing the buck." People will follow leaders almost anywhere as long as they have confidence that if the leaders make a mistake and get into danger, they will admit it and lead them back into safety.

- Confidentiality means that sensitive matters entrusted to the leaders, or information which has come to the knowledge of the leaders, is in safekeeping.

- Loyalty means that the leaders will stick by their people, support them and defend them against criticism or attack.

Leaders Have to Trust Their People

Because of the mutuality of all relationships (that is, there has to be input from both sides), not only do people have to trust their leaders in order for the relationship to succeed, but leaders also have to trust their people.

We have already seen that trust means letting certain outcomes go out of our control and placing them at least partly into the control of others. It is usually temperamentally harder for leaders to do this, because they are accustomed to being in control. That is why it is often difficult to "lead the leaders."

This inability to trust is often seen when leaders have difficulty delegating responsibility and the power and authority that go along with that responsibility. When in a church or other organization, leaders reserve to themselves the final authority in case things go wrong, often the reason is that underneath it all, they do not trust other people. Mistrustful leaders are no more likely to gain trust than uncommitted leaders are likely to gain commitment.

When a Breach of Trust Occurs

When leaders fail in their leadership responsibilities, a breach of trust occurs, because people have trusted those leaders to fulfill their functions. That is not to say that every mistake on the part of leaders constitutes a breach of trust. However, some blunders may be so serious, or repeated failures so inept, that people lose confidence in their leadership capacity even when they are convinced of their sincerity.

There may be no moral blame attached to a leadership failure. It may simply be that the leaders are out of their element, or they lack the necessary experience, skill or training. But there may be real breaches of trust that involve moral blame or censure, as when leaders treat people unjustly or unfairly, or take advantage of their position for personal gain, or allow personal differences or conflicts among them to divide the church organization.

There is another important and often overlooked factor. When leaders are guilty of moral lapses or failures in their personal lives, there is, along with anything else, a breach of trust involved. A leader's private character can never be separated from his or her public character.

In Conclusion

There are clearly pitfalls in leadership that must be avoided. The greater the responsibility, the greater is the need for the people who have been given a trust to prove themselves faithful (1 Corinthians 4:2). This is all the more true for Christians, for "it is the Lord Christ you are serving" (Colossians 3:24).

Thankfully, we can look to Jesus Christ for a perfect model of trustworthy leadership, and follow Him, even as we lead others. Praise Him!

Study questions:

1. How is leadership always a position of trust?
2. To whom are leaders accountable or answerable?
3. What qualities are vital in a leader?
4. In what way do leaders have to trust their followers?
5. As a leader or as someone who trusts a leader, which issues stand out as ones on which you personally need to focus?

Tom Marshall, now deceased, came from a Baptist background and was one of the leaders in the charismatic renewal in New Zealand after he received the baptism in the Holy Spirit in 1961.

An accountant by training, he had always worked in a secular occupation, latterly teaching business management in a government educational institute, but at the same time also established and led churches and engaged in a worldwide teaching and writing ministry.

He founded Kapiti Christian Centre, an independent charismatic church in Raumati, New Zealand, established Servant Industries Trust, a non-profit organization engaged in employment training projects, was founding editor of the national magazine *Today's Christian* and set up and ran a consultancy business involved in career counseling.

He wrote a number of books, including *Understanding Leadership, Living in the Freedom of the Spirit, Right Relationships* and *Healing from the Inside Out,* together with many booklets and articles.

He traveled extensively in the Pacific, Europe, Asia and North America, teaching in Youth With a Mission schools, Bible colleges, conferences, churches and public and business seminars. His main contributions were in the areas of leadership training, relationships, the Spirit-filled life, counseling, healing, the Kingdom of God and spiritual warfare.